The
Galbraith
Viewpoint
in
Perspective

The Galbraith Viewpoint in Perspective

Critical Commentary on
"The Age of Uncertainty"
Television Series by:

William F. Buckley, Jr.
Albro Martin
Sidney Hook
Peter Duignan
Robert Conquest
J. Clayburn La Force
Herbert Stein
Bernard Brodie
Robert Hessen
Peter T. Bauer
Francine Rabinovitz
Ronald Reagan

Edited by
Gerald L. Musgrave

HOOVER INSTITUTION PRESS
Stanford University   Stanford, California

Hoover Institution Press

© 1977 by the Board of Trustees of the
   Leland Stanford Junior University

All rights reserved

International Standard Book Number: 0-8179-4212-2
Library of Congress Catalog Card Number: 77-92085
Printed in the United States of America

DESIGN AND TYPOGRAPHY BY TED LIGDA, REDWOOD CITY, CALIFORNIA

Second printing, 1979

Contents

Dr. Gerald Musgrave is a research fellow in the Domestic Studies Program of the Hoover Institution.

Editor's Introduction

Gerald Musgrave

In 1976, while researching a book about public televison, I learned of a series on economic issues to be written and narrated by Professor John Kenneth Galbraith. Since I myself am an economist, my curiosity was aroused. The series was being co-produced by the British Broadcasting Corporation, the Canadian Broadcasting Corporation, and in the United States by public television station KCET in Los Angeles. It involved a request by the co-producers to the Public Broadcasting Service for $721,481 in American tax money.

I eventually found that they had been granted the money on the strength of several elaborate proposals, one of which included the following statement:

> A short discussion piece will be produced for each program presenting information while providing opportunity for extended and alternative viewpoints on the crucial issues of the series. The best economists in America will be involved in this wraparound.

When I attempted to find out who these "best economists" would be, the wraparound became an administrative runaround. Much later I was told Galbraith was so good that no alternative viewpoints would be necessary!

I contacted everyone I could find in the Corporation for Public Broadcasting, which apparently has the responsibility to set high-level policy, and the Public Broadcasting Service, which acts more as a producer. There were long arguments that included much discussion of contractual obligations, particularly obligations to the American public.

My position was not helped by the fact that most of the work, begun in 1973, was now complete; indeed, the last program, "A Weekend in Vermont," had been taped in July 1976. Finally, it was decided that alternative viewpoints would have to be presented.

To my surprise, I was made a consultant to the series. In January 1977, KCET asked me to prepare a list of prospective commentators and their qualifications. In ten cases, my recommendations were accepted. Drs. Brodie and Rabinovitz were recommended by KCET. I should emphasize that the station was diligent in its attempts to sign the best available people. Having signed them, it did not attempt to modify or edit any of their opinions. This booklet contains the text of the commentaries which were aired at the conclusion of each episode.

College students can now view "The Age of Uncertainty" for credit. Professor Galbraith's book of the same title is being distributed by the Houghton Mifflin Company with a book of readings titled *Points of Departure* and a study guide, *Pathways*.

To what destination does Galbraith lead us? For many years, Professor Galbraith has been portrayed as a liberal, someone swimming in the main stream of political ideology. In fact, he is not a liberal. Many critics now charge Galbraith with adhering to socialist views—a fact which may be evident to sophisticated viewers of the series but not to everyone. His viewpoint is so unremittingly hostile to capitalism and so adulatory to statism that it appeared to me to be a travesty to allow his opinions to be portrayed as uncontroversial.

Unfortunately, Professor Galbraith's work is also flawed with distortions. For example, as William F. Buckley, Jr., points out in the commentary reprinted here, Galbraith apparently believes that conservatives are opposed in principle to disaster relief. Albro Martin believes that "The Age of Uncertainty" mocks and demeans American history. Sidney Hook, a lifelong student of Marxism, rejects Galbraith's view of Marx the economist. Was colonialism, as Galbraith believes, an unqualified failure? If it was, says Peter Duignan, then how do we explain such former colonies as the United States and Australia. The lesson of history, according to J. Clayburn La Force, is that governments, not bankers, cause inflation. J. M. Keynes, the apostle of deficit financing whose work is idolized by Galbraith, is revealed by Herbert Stein to be an economist whose ideas bequeathed us inflation as a way of life. Two of Galbraith's favorite whipping boys, corporate power and intergroup differences in income, are portrayed in a very different light by Robert Hessen and Peter Bauer. These are only some of the alternative viewpoints to be found in this booklet—viewpoints that were each limited to four minutes of television time. These commentaries should not be considered as complete rebuttals of the fifty-minute program. In the event the reader may want to pursue these issues, the authors have supplemented the commentaries with suggestions for additional reading.

Since I am not one of these authors, the reader may well ask if I, too, have a viewpoint. I do. I believe there is a real question whether public broadcasting should involve itself in the presentation of issues that have strong ideological and political overtones. If it does, however, then it must devise methods to guarantee an open and competitive market for ideas. An ideological debate, financed at the public's expense, should not be a monologue.

1 The Prophets and Promise of Classical Capitalism

William F. Buckley, Jr.

One thing that was never uncertain in our otherwise uncertain age was that Professor John Kenneth Galbraith, an avowed socialist, would take this opportunity, in his genial but mischievous way, to thread the beads of history so as to festoon, one more time, his lifelong mistress, the state. Consider the treatment you have just seen of the Irish potato famine, the responsibility for which is all but laid at the door of capitalist theory.

Who was the towering figure in Great Britain at the time? Not Trevelyan, but his superior, the Prime Minister Sir Robert Peel.

What was the cause for which Sir Robert Peel gave his political life?

It was the repeal of the Corn Laws, which repeal he finally forced through Parliament in June of 1846.

What were the Corn Laws? They were statist impositions on free trade, maintained in Great Britain by what today would be called the agricultural lobby—in those days dominated by the great land-owning families.

What was the effect of the Corn Laws?

They forbade, except at prohibitive levels, the importation *or the export* of grain for fear of undermining the domestic price structure.

Who was the sovereign figure in the great crusade against such tariffs and export barriers?

Adam Smith. His towering work, *The Wealth of Nations,* was above all a polemic for free trade. Great Britain at the turn of the century was suffocating under age-old mercantilist restrictions on free economic activity—such restrictions as, in the modern age, are associated with the regulators, price controllers, high taxers, and inflationists. In England the cost of building a small house in 1800 was *50 percent higher* than it otherwise would have been—because of the tariff imposed on foreign lumber.

What did the terrible refusal of the British government to rescue the Irish have to do with the principles of classical economics?

Nothing.

There is no conservative principle against disaster relief.

Professor Galbraith cites Malthus. Malthus was a prophet, not an ideologist. He looked at history and deciphered a dilemma. It is one with which we struggle even today. There is great hunger in the world today. And such hunger as is is mitigated by surplus. And that surplus, where it exists, is the result of a free economic order. That is why the United States has shipped $10 billion worth of food to socialist India during the past generation, and why even now Canada, Australia, and the United States, with our relatively free agriculture, prevent starvation in the two socialist superpowers, China and the Soviet Union.

The blight in Ireland was as much a natural disaster as the destruction of Pompeii, or the black plague, or the Lisbon earthquake. To associate it with the workings of capitalism—which in the nineteenth century began, painfully, to usher us into an age of abundance sufficient to make possible massive aid to those in need—reminds one of the parson who used to reproach the assembled worshipers for the poor attendance at church.

"There is every reason to remember how miserable the majority of the people still were [at the turn of the nineteenth century]," Professor Friedrich Hayek, the Nobel Prize–winning economist, tells us in his discussion of the socialist interpretation of history. "But we must not, long after the event, allow a distortion of the facts, even if committed out of humanitarian zeal, to affect our view of what we owe to a system which for the first time in history made people feel that this misery might be avoidable."

Few things in life are so striking as the difference between a dry, antiseptic assault—conducted in the hermetic luxury of a television studio—on the gradual evolution of a set of principles that have brought material comfort and freedom to millions, and the joyful participation in the constructive enterprise of helping to bring a measure of well-being to mankind by protecting it from the certainty of misery and tyranny under socialism.

Suggested Readings

Coase, Ronald. "Adam Smith and the Wealth of Nations," *Economic Inquiry*, vol. XV, no. 3, 309–25, June 1977. Clearly states the nature of the great man and his work.

Friedman, Milton. *Adam Smith's Relevance for 1976*. Ottawa, Ill.: Green Hill Publishers, 1976. The Nobel laureate relates Adam Smith's writing to contemporary issues including the Humphrey–Hawkins Bill, AMTRAK, television commercials, and Galbraith's "Age of Uncertainty."

Haggarty, John, ed. *The Wisdom of Adam Smith*. Indianapolis, Ind.: Liberty Press, 1976. Eloquent and enduring excerpts from *The Wealth of Nations* and *The Theory of Moral Sentiments*.

Machlup, Fritz. *Essays on Hayek*. New York: New York University Press, 1976. F. A. Hayek. *The Intellectuals and Socialism*. Menlo Park, Calif.: Institute for Humane Studies, reprint 1976. These sources may yield insight into why there is an age of uncertainty.

Marshall, Dorothy. *Industrial England, 1776–1851*. New York: Scribner's, 1973. A different historical perspective of the period from that presented on television.

McCord, Norman. *Anti-Corn Law League: Eighteen Thirty-Eight to Eighteen Forty-Six*. New York, Humanities, 2nd ed. 1968. A definitive work on the subject.

"1776: The Revolution in Social Thought." *Journal of Law and Economics*, vol. XIX, no. 3, October 1976. This special issue of the *Journal* is a bicentennial tribute to the thoughts of Jefferson, Gibbon, Bentham, Turgot, and Smith.

Schumpeter, Joseph A. *History of Economic Analysis*. New York: Oxford University Press, 1954, pp. 397–99. Contains a brief discussion of free trade and foreign relations from 1790 to 1870 and references to Richard Cobden and John Bright, two important leaders of the Anti-Corn Law League.

Sowell, Thomas. *Classical Economics Reconsidered*. Princeton, N.J.: Princeton University Press, 1974. A scholarly examination of classical economic thought and its importance.

William F. Buckley, Jr., is an author, editor, and lecturer. His early schooling was in England and France. While studying political science, economics, and history at Yale University, he was also an assistant instructor in Spanish. After completing his B.A. at Yale, he was associate editor of the AMERICAN MERCURY. *In 1955, Mr. Buckley founded* NATIONAL REVIEW, *and eight years later he began his weekly column, "On the Right," now syndicated in over 300 newspapers. He is the author of fourteen books and numerous articles on a wide variety of subjects and hosts a weekly television show, "Firing Line," carried by the Public Broadcasting Service as well as commercial stations.*

2 The Manners and Morals of High Capitalism

Albro Martin

The program you have just seen reminds me of the time when it was fashionable for witty political commentators like Professor Galbraith to ask about a certain candidate for office, "Would you buy a used car from this man?" The hard fact is that Galbraith's "personal view" of American business leaders in the late nineteenth century, witty as it may seem, is second-hand history indeed, for it is almost exactly the interpretation that was fashionable forty years ago.

Obviously, the myths that have just been served up as history are still very dear to some hearts. But—let the buyer beware. The real history of American business is an exciting and rewarding story, and over the last generation serious historians have made great progress in telling this story for the very first time. Let me recommend to you and to Professor Galbraith a few examples.

In the early 1950s, Allan Nevins—considered by many to be the greatest historian America has ever produced—brought out his big two-volume biography of John D. Rockefeller, based on unrestricted access to the records of the Standard Oil Company. It revealed a gentle but determined man whose successful fight for discipline and organization in a new American industry—petroleum—produced the miracle of cheap, high-quality kerosene. For the first time in the history of mankind, even the poorest family could afford to read after the sun went down. Consider what *that* meant to the rise of civilization. Interest in business history grew rapidly thereafter. In 1962 Alfred D. Chandler published a book called *Strategy and Structure*, which is still a best seller of its kind and has done more than any other book to explain the evolution of the modern corporation. In 1970 Joseph Wall published his magnificent biography of Andrew Carnegie, who came to America as a fourteen-year-old Scottish immigrant and helped to make cheap steel the chief ingredient of modern civilization. In 1976, after several exciting years of work in original documents, I published my own contribution to this literature—*James J. Hill and the Opening of the Northwest* —about the Canadian immigrant to the United States who began as a local coal dealer in St. Paul, Minnesota. Hill solved the badly muddled transportation problems of the great American Northwest and became the most important railroad leader in American history. These people, and many others less famous, provided more and better goods and services, at constantly lower prices, to a rapidly growing population. If this is what Professor Galbraith means by robbing the people, then these gentlemen were "robber barons" indeed.

What bothers me most about the program you have just watched is that it mocks the history of America, demeans it, makes it something to be ashamed of. We must be critical of the past, but we must also try honestly to understand what our predecessors were trying to accomplish and the obstacles they faced in an age that was as full of uncertainty as our own. Our hearts should leap up at the adventures these men— and a few women—enjoyed. Yes, *adventures*—for none of these people worked for money beyond a very early point in their careers.

Our young people today are hungry for adventure. They would be fascinated to learn how much adventure our ancestors found not in playtime at Newport, but in laying the foundations of what Professor Galbraith himself has called the "affluent society." The real story can give young people the strength for their own lives. Without it, there is little for them to build upon. Professor Galbraith's churlish view of the past robs young Americans of a valuable inheritance—their history.

Suggested Readings

GENERAL WORKS

Brewer, Thomas B., ed. *The Robber Barons: Saints or Sinners?* New York: Holt, Rinehart & Winston, 1970. A paperback book of short readings arguing for and against the "robber baron" stereotype.

Chandler, Alfred D., Jr. *The Visible Hand: The Managerial Revolution in American Business.* Cambridge, Mass.: Harvard University Press, 1977. A study of the evolution of the large-scale, diversified, and, integrated American corporation to 1920, by the leading historian of big business.

Kirkland, Edward C. *Industry Comes of Age.* New York: Holt, Rinehart & Winston, 1961; paperback ed., Quadrangle, 1967. The development of the American industrial economy from the Civil War to 1897, by the late Professor Kirkland, who was more knowledgable about American business than almost any other historian of his generation.

Porter, Glenn. *The Rise of Big Business.* New York: A.H.M. Publishers, 1975. A short paperback survey of the evolution of large-scale business enterprise.

Potter, David. *People of Plenty.* Chicago: University of Chicago Press, 1954; also in paperback. A short but powerful book on the role that relative affluence has played in the development of the American character.

Schumpeter, Joseph A. *Capitalism, Socialism and Democracy.* New York: Harper Bros., 1942; also in paperback. A charming, thought-provoking study of the various types of economic society and the conditions under which they have been or might be brought into existence; by the leading theoretician of entrepreneurship.

STUDIES OF INDIVIDUAL BUSINESS LEADERS
OR ENTERPRISES

Grodinsky, Julius. *Jay Gould: His Business Career.* Philadelphia: University of Pennsylvania Press, 1957. A painstaking, detailed study of Gould's major business ventures, which reveals that whether on purpose or not, he proved to be one of the most important agents of the rational structuring of American big business in the late nineteenth century.

Hidy, Ralph and Muriel Hidy. *Pioneering in Big Business: The Standard Oil Company, 1882–1911*. New York: Harper, 1952. The classic study of the problems that faced the American petroleum industry in its formative years, and how John D. Rockefeller and his associates solved them, creating the first large-scale manufacturing corporation.

Martin, Albro. *James J. Hill and the Opening of the Northwest*. New York: Oxford University Press, 1976. A detailed study of the entrepreneurial exploits of the man who solved the tangled transportation problems of the booming Northwest from the 1870s to the turn of the century, and who became the most influential railroad leader in the nation. Based on Hill's complete papers, the best collection of the papers of any American businessman.

Nevins, Allan. *Study in Power: John D. Rockefeller*, 2 vols. New York: Scribner's, 1953. A landmark in the serious study of the careers of American business leaders, which has rendered obsolete the work of superficial writers like Matthew Josephson. (Also published in a one-volume abridgement by William Greenleaf.)

Wall, Joseph F. *Andrew Carnegie*. New York: Oxford University Press, 1970. The definitive study. Harold Livesay's *Andrew Carnegie and the Rise of Big Business* (Boston: Little Brown, 1975) is a well-written, much shorter study, which makes full use of Wall's research.

Albro Martin is a professor of business history at the Harvard Graduate School of Business Administration, where he is editor of the BUSINESS HISTORY REVIEW. *After graduate work in economics at Harvard, he entered business and spent seventeen years in marketing, advertising, and consulting, capped by ten years as an account research supervisor at the J. Walter Thompson Company. At the age of forty-four he returned to graduate school, taking a Ph.D. in history at Columbia University in 1970. He is the author of numerous articles and two widely acclaimed books—* ENTERPRISE DENIED: ORIGINS OF THE DECLINE OF AMERICAN RAILROADS, 1897–1917, *which won the Allan Nevins Prize in American Economic History, and* JAMES J. HILL AND THE OPENING OF THE NORTHWEST, *the definitive biography of one of America's great railroad magnates.*

3 | Karl Marx — The Massive Dissent

Sidney Hook

I want to focus on what Professor Galbraith calls the legacy of Marx—the Russian Revolution and the theory of historical materialism, which he mis-calls economic determinism. This is a strange legacy, for the Russian Revolution disproved the theory of historical materialism. Economic institutions in Russia in 1917 did not determine political thought and action. On the contrary, those who called themselves Marx's disciples first seized political power and *then* sought to build the collectivist economy in the last country in the world in which Marx expected it to come.

The Communists under Lenin actually nullified the theory of historical materialism because they showed that in the twentieth century the mode of political decision can be more important than the mode of economic production—that political action largely determines the nature of the economic system.

The failure of Marx's economic theories about development of capitalism in the West is also evidence of his defective legacy. He predicted the pauperization of the working class. Yet the workers reached levels of affluence never attained before. He predicted the disappearance of the middle classes and the polarization of society between a handful of plutocrats and the impoverished masses. But the middle classes still flourished and, politically, Main Street today is at least as important as Wall Street. Marx said that the workers have no fatherland and predicted they would never fight for home and country. But they have always fought. He predicted that the Socialist Revolution would first come in the highly industrialized West. It actually came where his own theories declared it impossible, in the most backward countries of the world.

On the other hand, Marx failed to predict what did happen—the rise of totalitarianism and the emergence of the welfare state. Some legacy!

Where did Marx go wrong? In his failure to realize the importance of the democratic political process in reshaping the economic system of capitalism and redistributing social wealth more equitably through tax and welfare measures. He failed to see that the so-called inevitable iron laws of economics and history could be bent by human will and intelligence.

Marx's true legacy was not his dubious economics, but his commitment to human freedom and dedication to human rights. He fought for the extension of democracy not only in the political sphere but in all other areas to reduce the tyranny of man over man and to further what today we call democracy as a way of life. He was an ardent opponent of all despotisms and bitterly denounced those who would impose dictatorship of a minority party over the working class. The emancipation of the working class, he asserted, can only be achieved by the working class itself—not by dictators.

There is a historical irony and a double paradox in the life and thought of Karl Marx. The irony is that although he contended that how a man earns his living explains how he acts and what he believes, how Marx himself acted and what *he* believed could never be explained by how he earned his living or by any economic conditions whatever—and this goes for Engels as well and their chief followers. The double paradox is that although Marx discounted the place and efficacy of moral ideals in history, without them neither he nor the movement he inspired would have left their mark on history. Today, in the countries in which Marx is revered, his ideals of freedom have been trampled into the dust. Only in the democratic welfare states of the West have Marx's ideals some hope of realization.

Suggested Readings

Acton, H.B. *The Illusion of the Epoch: Marxism-Leninism as a Philosophical Creed.* London: Routledge and Kegan Paul, 1973. Paperback. A vigorous criticism of Marxism as a philosophical creed, particularly the doctrines of dialectical and historical materialism, and of the Marxist ethics.

Bernstein, Eduard. *The Presupposition of Scientific Socialism* (English translation: *Evolutionary Socialism*). New York: Schocken Books, 1961. The classical work of the first great revisionist of Marx whose insights have been vindicated by historical events, and whose stature as a courageous critic and man of humane vision has grown with the years.

Crosland, C. A. R. *The Future of Socialism.* Westport, Conn.: Greenwood Press, 1977. One of the best expositions of an undogmatic, non-Marxist theory of socialism which stresses the ethical values of socialism.

Hook, Sidney. *Political Power and Personal Freedom.* New York: Macmillan, 1962. A series of essays on socialism, democracy, and civil liberties exploring among other things the extent to which a mixed socialist society or welfare state can be developed on the basis of personal freedom.

—————. *Revolution, Reform and Social Justice.* New York: N.Y.U. Press, 1975. An evaluation of some recent development in the theory and practice of Marxism.

Lichtheim, George. *Marxism: A Historical and Critical Study.* 2nd ed. New York: Praeger Publishers, 1964. A scholarly exposition of the development of Marx's ideas and the Marxist movement from 1848 to 1948.

McLellan, David. *Marx before Marxism.* New York: Harper and Row, 1970. An informative but uncritical biography of Karl Marx, more concerned with the details of Marx's personal life than with his basic ideas. (It seems to be the chief source of Galbraith's knowledge of Marx.) A more significant intellectual biography, although skimpier in gossipy details, is still Franz Mehring's *Karl Marx* (Berlin: Dietz Verlag, 1974.)

Russell, Bertrand. *Bolshevism: Practice and Theory.* New York: Harcourt,

Brace & How, 1920. One of the earliest expressions of disenchantment with the Russian Revolution of October 1917.

Schumpeter, Joseph. *Capitalism, Socialism, and Democracy.* New York: Harper and Row, 1970. Paperback reprint. A reflective and strikingly original analysis of the issues arising from the triumph and weakness of capitalism and its civilization.

4 The Colonial Idea

Peter Duignan

In contrast to Professor Galbraith, I do not believe that colonialism was a failure. It only appears so in such places as India or Algeria. But think of where it has been a great success—in the United States, Canada, Australia, and most of Latin America and Africa.

Colonialism was extremely effective in diffusing modern science and technology to backward societies. Wherever they went, the imperialists built the economic infrastructure of roads, harbors, and railways. They brought medical and educational services, modern agriculture, and mining. The colonialists created the museums, archives, libraries, research institutes, universities, and schools found in every colony.

The end of colonialism was not invariably messy nor was the departure usually sudden. Blood was not spilled more often than it was spilled during the imperial sunset. The French gave up rule in black Africa amicably in fifteen colonies and with only a little shouting and taking back of telephones and filing cabinets in one (Guinea). The British departed with grace and dignity from nine African colonies.

It is not a myth that men undertook colonialism for high moral reasons. Certainly private persons, joint-stock companies, and business groups took over large areas of the world for profit. Still, modern colonialism was overwhelmingly noncommercial minded. Missionaries went overseas by the thousands and died at a higher rate than soldiers in combat. Humanitarians and missionaries were the primary pressure groups pushing reluctant and skeptical European parliaments into acquiring colonies: "end the slave trade," cried the humanitarians; "spread Christianity," pleaded the missionaries; "stop tribal warfare," they both demanded. This was not using a pious purpose as a cover story, as Galbraith claims. The evidence clearly shows that colonies did not attract many capitalists, businessmen, or investors. What they largely attracted were missionaries and colonial officials.

The rallying cry of colonialism since the 1860s was the three "C's"—Christianity, commerce, and civilization. Bankers and industrialists did not put pressure on governments to acquire colonies so that they could make super profits. Few super profits were made in the colonies—even gold only returned an average profit of 6 percent per year from 1880 on. In Africa and Asia there were not great riches to be won, but poverty and underdevelopment to be overcome. It always took a great deal of money to administer and develop distant lands.

If capitalists did not lust for empire, neither did the masses. The citizens of Paris attacked the French National Assembly in an effort to lynch the minister who had acquired Indochina.

But the greatest error in Galbraith's presentation is in equating U.S. involvement in Vietnam with colonialism. We never controlled or ruled South Vietnam. We were invited in to help defeat a communist movement. We were in Vietnam on the same basis as the Cubans are in Angola, yet no one charges Cuba with colonialism in Angola. Vietnam did not represent the defeat of U.S. colonialism, but rather the victory of North Vietnamese communistic imperialism.

In my view, the balance sheet of European colonialism is positive; it did more good than harm. The colonialists imposed peace and law and order; they created larger political units or states out of scores of warring tribal polities; in Africa they ended the slave trade, slavery, and inter-tribal wars. European domination brought in its train good government, some education and medical services, roads and railways, ports and bridges, dams and canals. Africans acquired a multitude of new jobs and skills; they had more freedom than under their traditional rulers; they had more opportunities. An enormous transfer of skills and techniques transformed tribal societies and linked them to the world market.

Everywhere, colonial governments were small, efficient, and honest. Never have so many people been ruled so well by so few with so little fuss as during the colonial period in India and Africa, for example. The successor states have mostly become one-party dictatorships or are ruled by the military.

Colonialism had to end. All people have the right to rule themselves. But Professor Galbraith's account is unhistorical and distorts the record. On balance, colonial rule benefited the colonized. I agree with Karl Marx, who said it was a progressive force drawing backward societies into civilization.

Suggested Readings

GENERAL WORKS

Fieldhouse, D.K. *The Colonial Empires: A Comparative Survey from the Eighteenth Century.* New York: Dell Publishing Company, 1971.

Frye, Richard N. *The Near East and the Great Powers.* Cambridge, Mass.: Harvard University Press, 1951.

Gann, L. H. and Peter Duignan. *Burden of Empire: An Appraisal of Western Colonialism in Africa South of the Sahara.* Stanford, Calif.: Hoover Institution Press, 1971. Called by Britain's leading imperial historian, C. E. Carrington, "the first mature and comprehensive book on colonialism that has come out of America."

Lewis, Bernard. *The Middle East and the West.* Bloomington, Ind.: Indiana University Press, 1964.

Mason, Philip (pseud. Philip Woodruff). *The Men Who Ruled India.* 2 vols. New York: St. Martin's Press, 1954. Excellent account of the British conquerors and rulers of India.

NOVELS AND BIOGRAPHIES ILLUSTRATIVE OF IMPERIALISM

Cary, Joyce. *Mister Johnson.* London: Longman, 1975. Comic-tragedy about the relation between an African clerk and a British district officer.

Durrell, Lawrence. *The Alexandria Quartet,* 4 vols. I. Justine; II. Balthazar; III. Clea; IV. Mountolive. Very good on the mood of imperial rule in the Middle East.

Gibson, Charles. *Spain in America.* New York: Harper and Row, 1968. Good, readable survey of the Spanish empire.

Hanke, Lewis. *The Colonial Experience.* Boston, Mass.: Little, Brown, & Co., 1973. Excellent account of Spanish colonialism and how it transformed the people of the Americas.

Huxley, Elspeth. *The Flame Trees of Thika.* New York: Pyramid Publications, 1973. A beautifully written autobiographical account of the author's life in East Africa, from her childhood.

5 | Lenin and the Great Ungluing

Robert Conquest

The main weakness of Professor Galbraith's spirited presentation lies in the old-style economic and class basis he finds for his historical interpretation; its main strength, in the occasional passages where he breaks free from such a formula.*

He generalizes a scenario of "feudalism" and "capitalism" for Europe. Employed with discretion, such concepts can be useful. But Galbraith uses them in a rather coarse merger of populist and Marxist myth, common enough in the 1920s and 1930s, but now largely abandoned in serious circles in favor of a wider perspective—a consideration of the totality of social, historical, political, psychological, and economic circumstances. It is curious that just when he is presenting a particularly weak point, he asserts that it is now accepted by all "sensitive" students —I mean the old canard that Anglo-German trade rivalry was a main cause of the war. The Germans, of course, hoped to the last that Britain would not be among their enemies.

Then he attributes all the errors of World War I generalship to the supposed "caste" position of the generals. This was largely true of the German high command, only partially true of the Russian and British, and untrue of the French—who did none the better for that.

The disadvantage of prefabricated ways of looking at history is that

---

* Apart from the fallacy—and incoherence—of his main argument, Galbraith deduces so many of his facts from his opinions, instead of (as is preferable) vice versa, that in four minutes I could give only a few illustrations. With more time I would have pointed out, for instance, that his account of Lenin's peasant policy is wrong in three ways—on its timing, its content, and its results.

they exempt you from mere fact. So Galbraith writes offhandedly of Pétain—perhaps because he later became a "reactionary" leader—that he was one of the stupid generals. In fact, Pétain was one of the most uniformly successful. Again, he sneers at royalty and their nonbelligerent offspring. Britain's own King George V's "offspring," the future George VI, served as an ordinary midshipman and, as a sixteen-year-old, went through the superbattle of Jutland with warships blown to pieces all around him.

All this leads to a more-than-Marxist misunderstanding of Lenin's position, especially as regards the "workers." Lenin thought of himself as in some sense representing the proletariat, though he was always quite clear that the real workers could not be trusted except under strict control.

As Marxists are the first to point out, we should look at what politicians are actually doing, not what they think, or say, they are doing. Fewer than 2,000 workers were involved in Lenin's coming to power; and the minutes of his own Central Committee are frank about the lack of worker support. He later gained much worker support, for a brief period, by promises. But this had almost entirely evaporated by 1921, again on the Bolsheviks' own admission.

"We have failed," he said, "to convince the broad masses." In fact, what Lenin inaugurated, like other messianic revolutionaries before him, was an elite despotism over workers and others alike, dressed up in up-to-date phraseology.

Professor Galbraith concludes with his pet theory that Soviet and Western societies must inevitably "converge," owing to certain supposed parallels in economic organization. Here again he takes the single thread rather than examining the totality of historical, ideological, and other motivations. Recently Galbraith's views on this came under particularly sharp attack from Ota Sik, the former economic minister in Dubcek's brief liberal communist regime in Czechoslovakia. Which may remind us that the last word about Eastern Europe is not that it is as Galbraith has it—where empire collapsed—but rather where a new empire came into being.

Suggested Readings

Balabanoff, Angelica. *Impressions of Lenin*, tr. Isotta Cesari. Ann Arbor: University of Michigan Press, 1964. Valentinov, Nikolay. *Encounters with Lenin*, tr. Paul Rosta and Brian Schapiro. New York: Oxford University Press, 1968. Both are penetrating firsthand accounts.

Conquest, Robert. *V. I. Lenin.* New York: Viking Press, 1972. Concise and comprehensive.

Lafore, Laurence. *The Long Fuse: An Interpretation of the Origins of World War One.* Philadelphia: J. B. Lippincott Co., 1965.

Luxemburg, Rosa. *The Russian Revolution & Leninism or Marxism?* Ann Arbor: University of Michigan Press, 1961. Some of the most interesting pieces critical of Lenin from a Marxist viewpoint.

Schapiro, Leonard. *The Communist Party of the Soviet Union.* New York: Random House, 1960. The best conspectus of Communist Party history, which up to 1920 is very largely that of Lenin and his decisions.

Schapiro, Leonard and Peter Reddaway, eds. *Lenin: the Man, the Theorist, the Leader.* New York: Praeger, 1967. A most useful collection of essays (see, in particular, Peter Reddaway on Lenin's attitude toward the arts and Alec Nove on Lenin as an economist).

Ulam, Adam B. *The Bolsheviks.* New York: Macmillan, 1965. One of the best accounts of Lenin's career.

Robert Conquest, currently a senior research fellow at the Hoover Institution, was educated at Winchester College and Magdalen College, Oxford (M.A., D.Litt.). He served through the war in the British infantry and afterwards in the British diplomatic service. He is a former fellow at the London School of Economics, Columbia University, and the Woodrow Wilson International Center for Scholars. He holds the Order of the British Empire and is a fellow of the Royal Society of Literature. His books include several volumes of verse, a science fiction novel, and numerous scholarly studies on the Soviet Union, including THE GREAT TERROR *and* V. I. LENIN.

6 The Rise and Fall of Money

J. Clayburn La Force

Economists will be pleased by Professor Galbraith's generous and accurate treatment of Irving Fisher, who indeed was one of our country's greatest scientific economists. However, had Professor Galbraith presented the segment on Fisher early in the program, some of his vignettes would have taken on greater meaning and significance, for several of his historical examples beautifully illustrate the validity of Fisher's equation of exchange: that an increase in the amount of money will cause prices of most things to rise.

The Royal Bank of France is an example. When John Law started the bank in 1716 it was a private joint-stock company with a royal charter—then, two and one-half years later, the French regent bought out the private stockholders and, in effect, made it a government bank. In the next eighteen months it issued over 2.5 billion livres in notes, an enormous avalanche of paper representing sixteen times more than it issued as a private institution and more than twice the money in all of France in 1716. The effect of this huge increase in money on prices was dramatic. Prices in Paris jumped—they about doubled. When the crash came in May the populace rejected the bank's paper money, the money supply drastically and suddenly fell, and prices plummeted.

In contrast to the Bank of France's sad experience under government ownership, the Bank of England evolved into an unrivaled financial institution. From its inception in the late seventeenth century until recently, it was a *private institution*—owned by private stockholders and administered by their directors, though it performed the functions of a central bank. After 250 years of private ownership—a spectacular period for Great Britain—the Bank of England was nationalized in 1946, an act symbolizing the beginning of Great Britain's present melancholy economic era.

One of history's profound lessons is that great inflations inevitably are products of government actions rather than the actions of nefarious bankers.

Dr. Galbraith's witty treatment of banking development in the United States perpetuates incorrect interpretations of economic history and analysis. For example, he paints a dim picture of the entire industry of the pre–Civil War period by asserting that "the best documented story of this era is of the backwoods banks of Michigan." Wrong! Those wildcat banks were far, far from typical and are not the best documented—only the most outlandish and sensational. Of course, there were fraudulent banks, they existed, but usually in the sparsely populated and economically unsophisticated regions of the frontier. But the great majority operated efficiently and safely—even by today's banking standards. Witness the splendid and sophisticated financial centers in New Orleans and New England. Indeed, there is overwhelming evidence that people understood the various risks involved when using banks and that they also recognized the significant benefits of the services they obtained from these banks. They were not dullards being conned again and again by carnival barkers posing as respectable financiers.

Since it was a competitive banking system, customers usually had numerous alternative banks from which to choose, and in such an atmosphere honesty and efficiency were essential characteristics for the survival of a bank. Rather than demeaning the banking system of the pre–Civil War years, we should be aware of its contributions to our magnificently productive economic system of today. Indeed, fractional reserve banking was one of the important economic innovations of all time; it performs an enormously productive role in our economies by greatly reducing the costs of money and the exchange of commodities, and by bringing together and allocating savings for investment by borrowers.

Finally, our banking system has been and is characterized by honesty. There certainly are no more frauds amongst bankers than among other professionals such as lawyers, physicians, and, for sure, professors of economics.

Suggested Readings

Clough, Shepard B. and Charles W. Cole. *Economic History of Europe.* Boston, Mass.: D. C. Heath and Co., 1952. For discussion of the Bank of England and the Bank of France, see pp. 278–84.

Clough, Shepard B. and Richard T. Rapp. *European Economic History: The Development of Western Civilization*, 2nd ed. New York: McGraw-Hill, 1975. For discussion of the Bank of France and the Bank of England, see pp. 189, 190–91, 476.

Gunderson, Gerald. *A New Economic History of America.* New York: McGraw-Hill, 1976. For discussion of banking in the United States up to the creation of the Federal Reserve System, see chaps. 7 (pp. 183–94) and 12 (pp. 344–50).

Hammond, Bray. *Banks and Politics in America from the Revolution to the Civil War.* Princeton, N.J.: Princeton University Press, 1957. This is a useful general discussion of early American banking.

Wright, Chester W. *Economic History of the United States.* New York: McGraw-Hill, 1949. For discussion of banking in the United States up to the creation of the Federal Reserve System, see chaps. 15, 24, 39.

J. Clayburn La Force is chairman of the Department of Economics at the University of California, Los Angeles, and the author of numerous scholarly papers on economic history. One of his special interests is the economic history of Spain, and he is a prominent scholar in this field. He is also the coauthor, with Professor W. C. Scoville, of a five-volume work, THE ECONOMIC DEVELOPMENT OF WESTERN EUROPE.

7 | The Mandarin Revolution

Herbert Stein

J. M. Keynes was a great economist and he lived a fascinating life. Galbraith tells his story very well, although he romanticizes by describing him as an outsider struggling against odds. In fact, Keynes was a huge success in the intellectual and financial worlds.

Keynes helped to liberate us from the old dogmas of the gold standard and the balanced budget. But he left us with no substitute for these old rules except that we should do what is best for today.

The main trouble with this prescription is that what is best for today is often not best for the long run.

Galbraith doesn't quote Keynes's famous statement that "in the long run we are all dead." In those words, Keynes belittles the importance of thinking about the future. That is a great heresy for an economist. People in general tend to give the future too little weight, not too much. It is the duty of economists to remind us of the long-run consequences of our actions.

Thirty years after his death we are living in what would have been the long run to Keynes. And while we enjoy benefits from his teaching, we also suffer some evils from it.

Most important, we suffer the evil of inflation. It is no coincidence that the Age of Inflation follows the Age of Keynes. By teaching us that budget deficits are not always a sin, he inspired the belief that they are never an evil. By teaching us that government deficits could sometimes reduce unemployment, he inspired the belief that the economy could always be pumped up to higher and higher levels of activity by bigger and bigger deficits. The result of acting on these beliefs has not been full employment; it has been an uncomfortable combination of high unemployment and high inflation.

One may say that our excesses were not the logically necessary consequences of Keynes's ideas. But they were the probable results of those ideas in the real world. Keynes did not get along well with politicians, including Roosevelt and Churchill. He thought that they didn't know much economics, and he was right about that. But they may have known something that he didn't know—that in the arena where decisions are made, ideas have consequences that are not dreamt of in the classroom.

Galbraith thinks that he discovered, while running price control in World War II, that Keynesian policy would not check inflation and that the needed remedy is permanent price control. However, some of those stuffy, conventional men whom Galbraith laughs at recognized the connection between Keynesian policy and inflation long before Galbraith did. They foresaw that Keynesian policy would not only *not* check inflation, but would actively cause inflation. And they didn't believe that the inflation problem could be solved by price controls.

Galbraith has understandable nostalgia for the days when he commanded an army of 17,000 price controllers. I don't know of anyone else who wants to relive that experience, perhaps because no one else still around enjoyed it from such an exalted position. There is no evidence that price control stops inflation, at least outside the police states. Our solution will have to be found in a new combination of Keynesian insights with the old-fashioned virtues of self-restraint and fiscal prudence that both Keynes and Galbraith found so amusing.

Suggested Readings

Fellner, William, ed. *American Enterprise Institute Studies on Contemporary Economic Problems*. Washington, D.C.: American Enterprise Institute, 1976. A generally post-Keynesian view of the modern economy. See especially:

William Fellner. *Guide to the Volume*, pp. 1–16.

Phillip Cagan. *Monetary Problems and Policy Choices in Reducing Inflation and Unemployment*, pp. 17–54.

Herbert Stein. *Fiscal Policy: Reflections on the Past Decade*, pp. 55–84.

William Fellner. *Criteria for Demand Management Policies in View of Past Failures*, pp. 85–108.

Marvin Kosters. *Wages, Inflation, and the Labor Market*, pp. 109–62.

Gottfried Haberler. *The Problem of Stagflation*, pp. 255–72.

Friedman, Milton. "Nobel Lecture: Inflation and Unemployment." *Journal of Political Economy*, June 1977, vol. 85, no. 3, pp. 451–72.

Kosters, Marvin (with J. Dawson Ahalt). *Controls and Inflation*. Washington, D.C.: American Enterprise Institute, 1975. A factual study of United States experience in the 1970s.

Stein, Herbert. *The Fiscal Revolution in America*. Chicago: University of Chicago Press, 1969. A non-messianic history of the development of stabilization policy from Herbert Hoover to Lyndon Johnson.

Herbert Stein, economist and educator, received his undergraduate degree from Williams College and his Ph.D. from the University of Chicago. Dr. Stein has been an economic analyst and advisor to many governmental agencies and private research institutions including the Committee for Economic Development, the Brookings Institution, and the American Enterprise Institute. He was a member of the President's Council of Economic Advisers from 1969 to 1971 and its chairman from 1972 to 1974. He holds the A. Willis Robertson Chair of Economics at the University of Virginia. He is a regular contributor to the Wall Street Journal *and the Scripps-Howard Newspapers. Among his numerous writings, one of special relevance to this installment is* THE FISCAL REVOLUTION IN AMERICA *(University of Chicago Press, 1969).*

8 | The Fatal Competition

Bernard Brodie

Mr. Galbraith speaks of the "powerful warning" in what he calls "the most influential speech" of Dwight D. Eisenhower's career. He quotes the well-known passage about the "potential rise of misplaced power" in the "military-industrial complex." "We must never," the quote goes on, "let the weight of this combination endanger our liberties or the democratic process."

Well, this is a weighty pronouncement indeed, and it has been much quoted. But is it really true, or is it just plain bogy with a dash of bombast? Could it not be that the sense of this quotation greatly exaggerates the dangers?

We have lately seen exposed various kinds of corrupt behavior on the industrial side of that combination, including bribery both at home and abroad. The bribery is sometimes indirect and therefore not illegal, like the kind that sees a former Pentagon official, whether military or civilian, hired immediately upon his retirement by that firm whose product was the main subject of his oversight when he was still a servant of the government.

Now bribery is no doubt an evil thing. Still, it may be a long way from endangering our liberties or the democratic process. The corruption may be a matter of one company pushing its products over those of another company, or wanting to get some special leniency of treatment regarding cost overruns or the like, but that is usually as far as it goes.

No evidence supports the belief that any military-industrial complex played a part in getting us involved in Korea or Vietnam, let alone the two world wars. And insofar as that complex does have influence upon our choice of weapons systems, let's be clear which is the tail and which is the dog. The military do indeed play a powerful role in our government, mostly because many congressmen, among others, genuinely defer to their views or find it politically expedient to seem to do so. That can mean spending more money on armaments or, in the case of Vietnam, staying there longer than we otherwise might have. For while the military can hardly be blamed for our getting involved in that or any other war, once in, their instinct is always for what they call "mission accomplishment." In other words, they have a strong aversion to being tagged with failure, which in itself is hardly objectionable. But in these larger matters one does not see industry playing any significant part.

Much the same is true even in arms procurement. Rockwell International no doubt wants very much to sell the Air Force its B-1 bomber. It has therefore flooded congressmen with propaganda about the merits of this airplane and about the jobs that would be created from its manufacture. Still, if the country buys the B-1 it will not be because the company is eager to sell it, but because the U.S. Air Force is so desperately eager to have it.

And if the Congress and the Administration defer to the military on this or any other issue, it will be because of fears stimulated not by industry, but by our relations with the Soviet Union. As for the future of those relations, much naturally depends on what the Russians do, but even more on our interpretations of the intentions behind those actions. There are hostile interpretations of acts which are not in themselves hostile, and in my opinion Mr. Galbraith is usually on the right side when it comes to making these interpretations. But he should not confuse the picture by allusions to a conspiracy which is largely imaginary.

Suggested Readings

Brodie, Bernard. *War and Politics*. New York: Macmillan, 1973. Pp. 290–302, 318–34.

Proxmire, William. *Report from the Wasteland: America's Military-Industrial Complex*. New York: Praeger Publishers, 1970.

Rosen, Steve. *Testing the Theory of the Military-Industrial Complex*. Lexington, Mass.: Lexington Books, 1973.

Bernard Brodie received his Ph.D. in International Relations from the University of Chicago and was an associate professor at Yale University, senior staff member at the Rand Corporation, and professor at the University of California, Los Angeles. He is now professor emeritus from U.C.L.A. He is a fellow of the American Academy of Arts and Sciences and author of several books on military subjects; two of the best known are STRATEGY IN THE MISSILE AGE *and* WAR AND POLITICS.

9 | The Big Corporation

Robert Hessen

I am grateful for this opportunity to register my disagreement with the viewpoints presented by Mr. Galbraith. Much of his criticism of big business was vague and elusive—mere hints of evil and malfeasance. But he made one point quite explicitly: that there is something fundamentally wrong about the relationship between the shareholders and the corporate officers. So I want to focus my comments on that claim.

You were told that the corporate officers create and carry out corporate policy in collaboration with technical specialists in production, marketing, and finance. As a purely factual statement, it can hardly be faulted. But the show suggested that there is something improper: that the shareholders should have a more active voice or vote, and that if they don't, then their shares should be seized by the government and replaced with interest-bearing bonds.

I would like to point out that corporations are able to attract capital from investors precisely because the shareholders won't be required to play any active role in managing the enterprise. What investors seek is a *sideline* opportunity to earn profits on their money. Corporate shareholders, in other words, are deliberately and intentionally inactive.

Although the separation of ownership and control in giant corporations is frequently denounced, it merely represents a widening specialization of function, or division of labor. There is no reason why a shareholder must personally manage his own wealth instead of entrusting it to managerial specialists, as investors do when they become limited or silent partners, or buy mutual funds, or deposit money in savings banks, or purchase corporate bonds. None of these other opportunities carries *any* voting rights or voice in management. The primary safeguard for corporate shareholders, the most effective protection they possess, is their ability to instantly sell their shares if they are dissatisfied with the performance or policies of the officers. Through the mechanism of the stock market there is a daily plebiscite which allows shareholders to register their approval or disapproval.

Similarly, when corporations "go public" (when they sell shares to outsiders) the founding officers do not intend to surrender any of their managerial authority, and the new investors are never led to believe that they are acquiring managerial powers equivalent to those of general partners. For example, it seems perfectly obvious that when Walt Disney, or Edwin Land, the founder of Polaroid, or Thomas J. Watson of IBM sold stock in their companies to outsiders, they were seeking capital, not advice on how to produce cartoons, cameras, and computers. The shareholders earned their profits, based on their willingness to supply capital and take a risk. There was no guarantee that these companies would be successful, that they would continue to grow from small into giant corporations.

By what right and in whose name does anyone propose to expropriate the shareholders? If the relationship between investors and corporate officers is mutually acceptable and beneficial, if millions of people willingly invest their money in corporations which they personally will not manage, then government has no right to interfere or to deny shareholders their rewards when the companies prove to be successful.

It should never be forgotten that a corporation is a voluntary association among a group of individuals. Therefore, when you hear someone talk about taking away the rights of a corporation, please remember that person is really attacking individual rights.

Suggested Readings

Alchian, Armen A. and William R. Allen. *University Economics*, 2nd ed. Belmont, Calif.: Wadsworth, 1967. Ch. 15, "The Business Firm and Profits," pp. 247–66. A lucid exposition of why business firms exist and how they achieve their goals.

Baughman, James P., ed. *The History of American Management.* New York: Prentice-Hall, 1969. Scholarly essays on the rise of the professional managerial class in giant corporations.

Chandler, Alfred D., Jr. "The Beginnings of 'Big Business' in American Industry." *Business History Review*, vol. 33, Spring 1959, pp. 1–31.

Cochran, Thomas C. "The Business Revolution." *American Historical Review*, vol. 79, Dec. 1974, pp. 1449–67. Professors Chandler, Cochran, and Sears place the growth of big business in historical perspective.

Hessen, Robert. "Creatures of the State? The Case against Federal Chartering of Corporations." *Barron's*, May 24, 1976. A brief but far-reaching defense of corporations, including the separation of ownership and control.

Sears, Marian V. "The American Businessman at the Turn of the Century." *Business History Review*, vol. 30, Dec. 1956, pp. 382–443.

Slichter, Sumner H. "A Defense of Bigness in Business." *New York Times Magazine*, August 4, 1957. Reprinted in Paul Samuelson, ed., *Readings in Economics.* New York: McGraw-Hill Co., 1973. Argues that bigness does not preclude competition or innovation.

Robert Hessen is a historian educated at Queens College, Harvard University, and Columbia University. He taught in the Graduate School of Business at Columbia University until 1974. Since then he has been a research fellow at Stanford University's Hoover Institution and teaches in the Graduate School of Business. In 1977 he was designated as the Emma and Carroll Roush Scholar for American Studies. He is the author of STEEL TITAN: THE LIFE OF CHARLES M. SCHWAB *(Oxford University Press, 1975).*

10 Land and the People

Peter T. Bauer

The main theme of this show was that the most important cause of poverty lies in the relationship between land and people, that is, in scarcity of land or exploitation of cultivators. This is not so. For instance, amidst abundant land and vast natural resources, the Indians before Columbus remained wretchedly poor, without domestic animals and without even the wheel when much of Europe with far less land was already rich and had developed a very high culture. Incidentally, before Cortez the Aztecs commended in the show were very poor and practiced large-scale human sacrifice, which was not good for living standards, especially those of the victims.

Nor is the present Third World short of natural resources. Most of Africa and Latin America and much of Asia is sparsely populated. Many millions of extremely poor people have abundant cultivable land. Neither shortage of land nor exploitation accounts for the famines in thinly populated African countries such as Ethiopia and Tanzania. Even in India much land is officially classified as uncultivated but usable. The small size and low productivity of farms in much of the Third World reflect the want not of land but of ambition, energy, and skill, which also explains the low level of productive capital.

Before the mid-nineteenth century, when many of them had already become rich, Jews and non-conformists in Europe had neither land nor political rights. Again, the poor, illiterate Chinese immigrants in prewar Malaya were largely barred from owning land, but they nevertheless greatly outdistanced not only the privileged Malays but also the immigrant Indians—one of many examples of group differences in economic performance.

Sustained prosperity owes little or nothing to natural resources—witness, in the past, Holland, much of it drained from the sea by the seventeenth century; Venice, a wealthy world power built on a few mud flats; and now West Germany, Switzerland, Japan, Singapore, Hong Kong, and Taiwan, to cite only the most obvious instances of prosperous countries very short of land and natural resources, but evidently not short of human resources.

If poverty were inherently self-perpetuating, as is often argued and also suggested in the show, countless people would not have risen from poverty to riches all over the world, conspicuously so in the United States and the Far East.

Nor do income differences normally reflect exploitation, but differences in performance. Income and wealth are usually earned or produced, not extracted from other people by depriving them of what they had, or could have had. The way to look at income differences is this: some people and societies have emerged from the surrounding sea of poverty sooner or to a greater extent than have others, but the earlier emergence of the former helps rather than obstructs the performance and prospects of the latter.

Economic performance depends on personal, cultural, and political factors, on people's aptitudes, attitudes, motivations, and social and political institutions. Where these are favorable, capital will be generated locally or attracted from abroad, and if land is scarce, food will be obtained by intensive farming or by exporting other goods.

Poverty and prosperity are not usually matters of land. Poverty or riches, and personal and social satisfaction depend on man, on his culture, and on his political arrangements. Understand *that*, and you understand the most important cause of wealth or deprivation.

Suggested Readings

Bauer, Peter T. *Dissent on Development*. Cambridge, Mass.: Harvard University Press, 1976, paperback edition.

————. "Western Guilt and Third World Poverty." *Commentary*, January 1976.

————, and Basil S. Yamey. "Against the New Economic Order." *Commentary*, April 1977.

————. "Foreign Aid Forever." *Encounter*, March 1974.

Brunner, Karl, ed. *First World—Third World*. Rochester, N.Y.: Center for Research in Government Policy and Business, University of Rochester Press, 1977. Essays by Karl Brunner, Harry Johnson, and Peter T. Bauer.

As a whole, these works challenge the idea that economic growth in underdeveloped countries requires central planning. They demonstrate that there is no basis for the idea of a "vicious circle of poverty" which can only be broken by aid from the West. They not only show why foreign aid has not worked so far, but why it is neither necessary nor sufficient for economic development of Third World countries—and, indeed, in its present form is likely to be damaging to development.

Peter T. Bauer is an economist and educator, born and educated in Budapest, Hungary. He earned his master's degree at Gonville and Caius College, Cambridge, and was a fellow at that institution from 1946–1960. He was Woodward lecturer at Yale and Roush Distinguished Visiting Scholar, Hoover Institution, Stanford University. Currently he is Fellow of the British Academy and professor of economics at the London School of Economics. He has contributed to numerous professional journals and is the author of several books. Among these are: WEST AFRICAN TRADE (Cambridge, 1954 and London, 1963); INDIAN ECONOMIC POLICY AND DEVELOPMENT (1961); MARKETS, MARKET CONTROL AND MARKETING REFORM (1968), with B. S. Yamey; DISSENT ON DEVELOPMENT: STUDIES AND DEBATES IN DEVELOPMENT ECONOMICS (1972).

11 | The Metropolis

Francine Rabinovitz

Mr. Galbraith's discussion of the metropolis raises a point about our cities that few people understand. It is that public revenues are generated today in a place quite different from the place where public services are actually needed. The revenue-raising function is divorced from the point of revenue-expenditure decision. The federal and state governments are banks—some would say collection agencies. Their business is to loan or grant money to localities. For example, in California and New York in 1975 almost three-quarters of these states' own revenues were spent as transfers to local governments.

Why has this system developed? It exists because despite the overall growth of metropolitan areas, most inner cities are losing population and economic capacity while the demand for services increases. The average family moving into the inner core now has an income about $1,300 smaller than the average family moving out to the "Great Camp" in the suburbs. In the fifty largest inner cities there is a long-term mismatch between revenue potential and service demands. There is no realistic prospect that most of these cities can generate enough revenue to finance the bulk of services they need to provide in the future. This is not a new development. It has been evident since the mid-1930s. It is reflected in the fact that, on the average, more than 40 percent of big-city expenditures are now financed through federal and state taxes.

Yet the rhetoric that cities can live within their own means persists. It endures because we believe it is the only discipline on officials of inner cities not to give in to the extravagant expenditure demands. But its more important effect is to avoid the admission that we already have in operation a huge and unwieldy transfer mechanism to get money from the middle and outer rings of metropolises to areas where it is needed more—in the center. And it hides the fact that these mechanisms are neither temporary nor limited to special areas of federal or state concern. We do not like to admit we are making outright income transfers. This offends our sense of self-reliance. But we are even less willing to admit that we have structured our older metropolitan areas—walling off the financial strength of the suburbs from the inner cities except through the federal and state governments—to ensure that the older cores must receive such transfers to survive.

It is time to remove the myth that any large old city can be self-sufficient. For only then, when transfer mechanisms and transfer-dependent inner cities are recognized for what they are, can we improve the situation.

Any banker puts conditions on a loan; so, too, do federal and state governments. What may be needed is to demand productivity improvements in exchange for employee benefits, to place limits on salary increases through collective bargaining, or to monitor local budgets in return for funds. We could shorten the loop money now travels, just as we can now telephone from one West African country to another without routing the call through Paris. It may be necessary to match the transfer of funds to the maintenance of minimal standards of living. A vigorous public debate is needed to determine these standards.

Beyond the need for basic support to provide minimum services, there are other problems as well. We must also admit that nirvana will not result from incessant degradation of services and physical plant. For this purpose, the stimulation of private interest is critical. This category of problems, unlike inner-city transfer needs, can be dealt with through mechanisms designed to bring private market forces to bear.

Suggested Readings

Banfield, Edward. *The Unheavenly City Revisited*. Boston, Mass.: Little, Brown & Co., 1974. A striking essay designed to demonstrate that the principal causes of urban problems lie in the attitudes of "lower class" citizens, and that government programs have often contributed to city problems rather than to their solution.

Gorham, William and Nathan Glazer. *The Urban Predicament*. Washington, D.C.: The Urban Institute, 1976. A series of articles describing major urban problems including transportation, crime, housing and finance, and alternative options for government programs to solve them.

Wildavsky, Aaron and Jeffrey Pressman. *Implementation*. Berkeley, Calif.: University of California Press, 1973. A case study of the city of Oakland's attempt to implement an economic development program under federal auspices, graphically demonstrating the complexity of the process of turning good intentions into programmatic outcomes.

Wood, Robert. *1400 Governments*. Cambridge, Mass.: Harvard University Press, 1961. A description of the political economy of the New York metropolitan region which provides insight into the consequences of governing an area through governments divided into separate and warring fiefdoms.

Yates, Douglas. *The Ungovernable City*. Cambridge, Mass.: MIT Press, 1977. A first class introductory textbook on the nature of city politics, combining a viewpoint which emphasizes the importance of neighborhoods, the validity of the government "should-do-less" philosophy, and a series of graphic descriptions of how big city decisions are actually made with basic information on city demographic, economic, and institutional structures.

Francine Rabinovitz received her undergraduate degree from Cornell University, and her Ph.D. in political science from the Massachusetts Institute of Technology. She is currently Professor of Public Administration and Urban and Regional Planning at the University of Southern California. She is also vice president of Hamilton-Rabinovitz, Inc., policy research and management consultants. She is the author of several books and articles on a wide variety of topics concerned with urban politics and administration. Unlike a number of other commentators on Professor Galbraith's views, Dr. Rabinovitz is not in fundamental disagreement with his analysis of the basic problems of the cities. Her comments are designed to build from a similar viewpoint, practical recommendations for changes necessary to improve urban conditions, particularly in the larger cities, in the 1980s and beyond.

12 | Democracy, Leadership, and Commitment

Ronald Reagan

I've been watching "The Age of Uncertainty" with great interest. No one could accuse Dr. Galbraith of lacking either an interest in the broad sweeps of history or a sense of humor. Just the same, the program leaves me uneasy. Uneasy, partly because it uses skillful editing to glorify Dr. Galbraith's heroes and make those he disagrees with seem ignorant, unfeeling, or downright villainous. But more important, I am uneasy about his view of just what constitutes Democracy, Leadership, and Commitment.

Early in the program, he gives us a glimpse at Switzerland's federal democracy at work. He makes the point that it works because it is close to the people and the emphasis is on problem solving. "The money is spent by the people who pay," he says.

So far so good. That's an idea that worked pretty well in the United States until some people began getting the idea that they could make government solve every problem that came along, if only they were put in charge of its machinery.

Having allowed government to grow to monster size, we have produced a cadre of professional, lifetime politicians, most of whom ply their trade by periodically raising their constituents' hopes of solving the latest problem. Once reconfirmed by the voters, they always follow the same method, dispensing huge amounts of tax money, passing laws that lead to restrictive regulations, then blaming those they regulated when things break down. And *then*, passing more laws and regulations because things obviously don't work. The ruling class of politicians and bureaucrats we have been breeding for several decades benefits from bigger and bigger government. And the opposite side of *that* coin is, inevitably, less liberty for individual citizens.

Dr. Galbraith says that the essence of leadership is "to confront, without doubt or equivocation, the major aspiration, the greatest need, the gravest anxiety of the people you presume to lead." He cites Nehru, Franklin Roosevelt, and John Kennedy as models. But there is something lacking in his definition. Essential also to leadership, it seems to me, is a clear belief in the limitations of government, coupled with a strong faith in the ability of individual men and women to think for themselves and to make decisions for themselves.

As an academician, Dr. Galbraith understandably places emphasis on education's role in democracy. He says, "The greatest source of democratic power . . . derives from education." He adds that it helps bestow the self-confidence, the sense of purpose, the ability to identify with a people's anxieties. He then takes us to the University of California where much of the anti-Vietnam war movement began. He is impressed by the ability of that movement to change events as it did. He does not also show us its anti-intellectual, anti-democratic side when mobs rampaged through the streets of Berkeley and demonstrators wanted anything *but* free speech for those who opposed them.

The impression comes through in this program that leadership is best left to development by a group of wise mandarins on college campuses. We can forgive Dr. Galbraith this bias in favor of his own profession, but the mandarins did not stop the violence. In fact, some even encouraged it in those days. And today, many of their products enter public service with the view that man was meant to be just an ant in society's anthill.

In the last analysis, Dr. Galbraith and I have different views of man and his relationship to society and government. He extolls the submersion of personality and self-interest in what he says is being "part of the team." I am suspicious of people who profess to have no self-interest, only that of the group or community.

Dr. Galbraith seems to believe that it is a simple matter to identify what the community interest is. I am afraid that he forgets that the community interest is constantly subject to the reality of pressure from special-interest groups of all kinds. Leaders will act in terms of what they *believe* is the main anxiety of their constituents, but they are far from being always right. As often as not, it is the squeakiest wheel that gets the grease.

Rather than government-by-squeaky-wheel, history has shown us that it is better to leave the individual alone to develop to the fullest extent possible whatever talents God gave him. As for leaders, give us those who know the difference between what society as a whole—and government—can and should do, and what it should leave alone.

Suggested Readings

Beichman, Arnold. *Nine Lies about America*. New York: Library Press, 1972. A sharp rebuttal to the New Left's condemnation of American civilization.

Friedman, Milton. *Capitalism and Freedom*. Chicago, Ill.: University of Chicago Press, 1962. A modern classic. The first chapters discuss the role of government in a free society and the necessity of having economic freedom in order to have political freedom.

Kirk, Russell. *The Roots of American Order*. LaSalle, Ill.: Open Court, 1974. A conservative's powerful statement on political science and law from a historical perspective.

Morley, Felix, ed. *Essays on Individuality*. Indianapolis, Ind.: Liberty Press, 1977. A reprint of an important collection of essays on the challenges to individualism. Includes contributions by F. A. Hayek, Richard M. Weaver, and Helmut Schoeck.

von Mises, Ludwig. *The Anti-Capitalistic Mentality*. South Holland, Ill.: Libertarian Press, 1972. Analyzes why capitalism is resented and attacked, most notably by intellectuals. If you enjoy this book you might read his much longer *Human Action* (Henry Regnery Co., 1966). Chapter 8 on peaceful cooperation or chapter 15 on freedom are of special interest.

Ronald Reagan is a businessman, rancher, and former governor of California. He received his B.A. in economics and sociology at Eureka College, Illinois, in 1932. He began his career as a sports announcer and later appeared in over fifty films for Warner Brothers and Universal Studios. During these years, he served as a member of the Board of Directors of the Screen Actors Guild and was its president for six terms. In 1966, he was elected governor of California and served two terms. Since leaving office in early 1975, Mr. Reagan has been giving a daily radio commentary on a national network and writing a syndicated weekly newspaper column. He was a candidate for the 1976 Republican nomination for president. Since the campaign, he has renewed his radio program and his newspaper column. He currently serves as chairman of a Republican-oriented political action organization, Citizens for the Republic.